Your First
FERRET

Adelle Porch

CONTENTS

Pages 2-3 and 34-35:
Photos by
Isabelle Francais

© 1991
By T.F.H.
Publications,
Inc., Neptune,
N.J. 07753 USA
— • —
T.F.H.
Publications,
The Spinney,
Parklands,
Denmead,
Portsmouth
PO7 6AR
England

Introduction

The ferret is an animal cloaked in mystery, although it has been kept in captivity for centuries. Countless stories are told about it from countryfolk. There was a time when thousands of people kept ferrets for rabbit hunting. A ferret was placed into a rabbit hole to chase the rabbits into the nets of hunters. Ferreting had a strong following in Wales, Scotland and northern England. Then came myxomatosis, the dreaded rabbit disease. It virtually wiped out the entire rabbit population. Ferreting never recovered from that event.

The ferret reached the New World via South America. Ferrets were taken on board sailing ships to keep down the mice and rat populations.

Hounds were the animal of the wealthy in the chase of deer, boar and other game. The ferret became the poor man's hound. It was easily housed and could be used on common land. Along with lurcher dogs, the ferret was kept by poachers, who ventured onto the estates of the rich to secure a few rabbits. Thus, the ferret became strongly associated with working people.

The ferret's reputation is rather unsavory. It is credited with being savage, smelly, bad-tempered and untrustworthy. Nothing could be further from the truth. A ferret can be docile, friendly and entertaining if handled correctly from an early age.

Ferrets are enjoying a resurgence in popularity today. Many are found as pets in homes. As the ferret shrugs off its old negative image, it is seen in its true light.

Like many other animals, ferrets have suffered at the hands of ignorant owners. This book is designed to give potential ferret owners a clear understanding of what they can and cannot expect of a ferret. A ferret is no more suited to all people than is a dog or cat. It is the wise person who finds out as much as he can about an animal before committing himself to the responsibility of owning it.

A ferret cannot be trained like a dog, nor can it be given the outdoor freedom of a cat. However, if you are looking for a more unusual pet, yet one not demanding intricate dietary needs and maintenance, the ferret may be for you.

A ferret is not a suitable pet for a household with young children. A ferret is not as mild-tempered as a dog or cat. If handled badly, a ferret will bite. However, an older child, one familiar with handling animals, can learn a lot about responsibility as a ferret owner.

A ferret can be kept safely with dogs and cats, providing there is a properly supervised period of introduction.

History

The ferret is the domesticated form of the European polecat, *Mustela putorius*. *Mustela* is Latin for weasel; *putorius* is from the Latin verb *putor*, to smell bad. This relates to the fact that polecats have scent glands from which they release a foul-smelling liquid as part of their defense mechanism. There is still debate as to which wild polecat is the ferret's ancestor. *Mustela putorius* is considered the most likely. The Russian species *Mustela eversmanni* is the second choice.

Many people think of the ferret as an all-white animal. This is because the albino is one of the most popular forms. However, ferrets can be purchased in a variety of colors, ranging from white to almost black. Indeed, color breeding is a strong reason why some people enter the hobby. In this respect, the ferret is in its infancy, yet it has much potential. There is no doubt that color forms have great appeal to pet owners. Therefore, much expansion is expected in this area.

CARNIVORES

The ferret belongs to the large order of animals known as Carnivora. The animals of this order range in size from the tiny dwarf weasels through to the largest land carnivore, the Kodiak bear. Between these extremes are many familiar species: lions, tigers, dogs, cats, seals and walruses. Although principally meat eaters, most carnivores are also secondary vegetarians, eating grasses, berries and fruits. A few, like the giant panda, are exclusively vegetarian.

Based on their similarities to a supposed common plan, or archetype, the carnivores are divided into a number of families. These include Ursidae (bears), Canidae (wolves, dogs) and Felidae (cats). The ferret is included in Mustelidae. This family contains animals such as otters, badgers, skunks, weasels, martins, grisons, wolverines, minks and ermines.

The mustelids are quite old. They were among the first mammalian types seen following the sudden disappearance of the dinosaurs during the Cretaceous period. During the next period, the Tertiary (also known as the Age of Mammals), most modern carnivores emerged. It is generally thought that the earliest carnivores of our times evolved from small animals, such as civets, which are regarded as living fossils. Civets are of the family Viverridae. They are similar to weasels in their general shape. This creates some confusion when tracing the history of the domestic ferret. It is probable that references citing weasels that were used to hunt snakes actually describe the mongoose, a viverrid.

In addition to the ferret, the genus *Mustela* includes the weasel, the mink, and the polecat. Photo by Isabelle Francais.

Ferrets have been maligned—unfairly—as rather unsavory little characters. Given the proper attention and care, a ferret can make a most endearing and entertaining pet. Photo by Isabelle Francais.

Housing

A tame, well-acclimated ferret will spend most of its time indoors at liberty. Even so, ferret keepers most often opt to provide a commercially bought cage or insulated box for their pets to take evening refuge. Pet shops offer a variety of durable, portable, easy-care cages for this purpose. All accommodations should be ready and waiting for the new residents, including an exercise pen, outdoor home, catchbox, etc.

EXERCISE PENS

The ferret kept as a household pet can benefit from the time it spends in an outdoor enclosure. A ferret can suffer from heatstroke, yet it enjoys short periods dozing in the sunshine. Therefore, exercise pens must take account of these two factors.

An outdoor pen should be as large as space and funds permit. A rectangular pen is better than a square pen of the same area size, since the ferret is able to run further along the length. Essentially, the run is a box shape made of welded wire.

For two ferrets, a good length is 15 x 4 x 3 ft 3 in (4.5 x 1.2 x 1 m). Construct three wooden frames to form the sides and top of the run. The timber should be solid, about 2 x 2 in (5 x 5 cm) or 2 x 1 in (5 x 2.5 cm). Smaller frames are needed at either end, or they can be of solid

timber .5 in (1.25 cm) thick. Cover the frames with welded wire of 1 x 1in (2.5 x 2.5 cm) hole dimensions and of strong gauge (at least 19G).

Bolt the frames together on their top edges. Then bolt the bottom edge onto a concrete slab floor or into a solid concrete floor. The bottom edges can also be given rigidity with wooden or metal cross members. Make a pophole in one of the end pieces so the two ends can be bolted onto the main structure.

A more portable unit can be assembled by using shorter frames, about 6.5 ft (2 m). If the pen is not to stand on concrete, then a fourth frame can act as a base. In this case, the unit can rest on lawn or bare earth. This basic unit can be modified to suit your particular needs.

For ease of access, the roof or a side panel can be hinged. If the unit contains a pophole, a simple slide-up shutter can be attached to close the pophole as desired.

The exercise shelter only needs to be a simple box bolted onto the pophole. It is a refuge in which the ferrets can sleep or avoid direct sun. It must be made of good, solid timber to provide insulation. The roof should be hinged.

A mini playland can be arranged within the pen. It is comprised of pipes, stacked logs, stones, a shallow pond and the like. The ferrets will amuse themselves for hours on end.

An even larger unit provides more scope, while a smaller unit is better than none at all. Such a unit can be unbolted if it needs to be moved, or it can be made into a permanent pen. It is also possible to fit similar pens to houses. Simply install a cat-flap door to your home. The ferrets can come and go as they please.

OUTDOOR FERRET HOME

The essentials of an outdoor ferret home are that it is dry, free from drafts and constructed of easily cleaned timbers. The dimensions should be generous. If these requirements cannot be met, do not keep ferrets permanently outdoors.

A good ferret home is comprised of three areas: a sleeping area, an exercise area and a toilet area. Feeding is normally done in the exercise area. Defecation is at the place furthest from the sleeping area. From this general arrangement, a number of permutations can be designed from a simple structure.

To avoid underfloor dampness and wood rot, construct the home on wooden leg supports. This also makes routine cleaning easier because you do not have to bend down. The dimensions required for two ferrets are a minimum of 5 x 1.5 x 2 ft in height (1.5 x .5 x .6 m).

The sides and top are made using .5 in (1.25 cm) thick tongue and grooved wood or chipboard. A thickness of .75 in (2 cm) is better for

the base, as it will be less prone to warping. Coat the inner surfaces with a gloss paint or emulsion impregnated with an acaricide. This discourages lice, fleas and other parasites from hiding in the crevices. The outside can either be painted or the wood treated with a colored wood preservative. Extend the roof beyond the sides for an overhang. Cover this with a roofing felt to make it waterproof. Give the floor several coats of paint to prevent staining and smelling by urine.

A nice extra in the toilet area is a hole cut in a corner of the floor. Cover this with welded wire mesh of .5 in (1.25 cm) hole size. Below this, fit a sliding drawer filled with sawdust. The feces fall through the mesh and into the drawer. The toilet area thus is easily cleaned and freshened.

The internal layout of the home should consist of a sleeping area on one end, the play area in the middle and the toilet at the other end. Each area should be separated by a solid wooden wall. Holes are made just large enough for a ferret to climb through. Alternatively, sliding partitions can be made.

The two end rooms should be fitted with externally opening solid doors to facilitate cleaning. The exercise area should have a wooden framed, welded wire mesh front. The mesh should be of stout gauge with 1 in (2.5 cm) hole size. This front can be hinged, though a totally removable door is easier for cleaning. A sliding shutter

If you want your pet to have a companion, but do not plan on breeding ferrets, it is best to select female animals: male ferrets (called hobs) sometimes can be fiercely aggressive in their attempts to establish dominance over fellow male ferrets. Photo by Isabelle Francais.

Ferrets come in a lovely variety of colors, including solid white. Photo by Isabelle Francais.

incorporated into the sleeping compartment, operated from the outside, allows you to shut the ferrets in one area while you are cleaning another.

FLOOR COVERING

Wood shavings, straw, and hay make suitable bedding material in the outdoor ferret home. The idea is to provide a material to soak up urine and moist feces. Sawdust and wood shavings are better for the play area and toilet; straw and hay are better for the sleeping area. Any wood product should be chemically untreated. Pine and other fragrant woods are best for controlling odor.

Straw should be clean and relatively dust free. Too much dust can cause eye problems. Hay is fine in moderation. During hot weather, however, hay can cause sweat rashes. Dried leaves are used by ferrets to make bedding nests. Shredded and granulated paper are available from most pet shops. This paper is free of printing ink, which, if swallowed, can cause stomach upset. Avoid stringy packing material used for china and glassware. These strands have sharp edges that can easily cut a ferret.

CATCHBOX

A useful extra on a ferret home is a catchbox. This is simply a small box fitted to the back of the home. It is large enough for one ferret to climb inside via an entry hole. The hole is opened and closed using an external shutter.

The catchbox can be solid wood with a plexiglass or solid lid. The front is welded wire. The catchbox allows you to easily lift out an individual ferret. The ferret can be enticed into the box with a tasty tidbit.

RAIN COVER

Another useful extra for a ferret home is a clear sheet of plexiglass .5 in (12 mm) thick. Drill holes in its corners and hang it over the front of the home during periods of driving rain or snow. It should not extend the full height of the mesh. This way it will not become soaked with condensation. Take it as high as the point which is protected by the overhang of the roof. It can be held in place at its bottom edge with simple butterfly swivel catches.

SITE

The site for the ferret home is important. It is best placed where your ferret can enjoy the early morning sun, yet still have protection from the elements. Near a wall or under an overhead awning is ideal.

CLEANING

The housing must be cleaned on a regular basis. The minimum is once a week—more often for smaller accommodations. The use of a mild disinfectant is recommended. However, be sure the home is dry before replacing the ferrets after cleaning. Change the bedding regularly. Food dishes must be cleaned daily.

The Pet Ferret

It is important to discuss the purchase of a ferret with the entire family. Assure all members that a ferret is neither dangerous nor smelly. It certainly is not noisy! A ferret is playful, even mischievous. It can be house trained in much the same way as a cat. Its feeding routine is simple. And as an extra bonus, any mice in the home will be long gone!

A ferret can get along just fine with a dog or cat—subject to an introductory period. About the only drawback is that a ferret cannot be allowed to roam loose outdoors. You will never see it again.

Ferrets are hoarders. This means that your pet may take an article and hide it in an unusual spot. Ferrets are also "nappers." They will curl up anywhere, from the cupboard to your bed, to take a snooze. Since a ferret is so lithe, it can get itself into trouble. If your pet is not in sight, check open drawers and cabinets. Otherwise, your ferret may be shut in for many hours.

Your ferret may curl up in your lap for some stroking. It may even be taken for a walk on a leash and harness.

BITING

A ferret is comparable to a cat in many ways. Some ferrets are as benign. Others really enjoy handling, some less so. The important thing is to not mishandle a pet. Generally, a ferret treated well and handled often from a young age is quite tame. Problems occur only if the ferret is treated roughly.

AGE TO BUY

The younger the ferret the better, providing it has been weaned. This means that an ideal ferret is about eight weeks old. If possible, choose one from a litter which has been handled regularly by its breeder. There is no shortage of ferrets, so there is no reason to consider an older animal.

Observe a number of ferrets before committing yourself to one. Find out if there is a local ferret club. Attend a meeting. Ferret owners will be happy to talk about the joys and responsibilities of ferrets. Most probably a member will have a pet with a litter due or available.

WHERE TO BUY

The ideal point of purchase is a pet shop. These animals have received the required inoculations. Also, it is likely that all the accessories can be purchased at one stop.

Check the living conditions at the pet shop. The ferret accommodations should be clean. The personnel should be knowledgeable and the store well stocked.

Ferrets are avid and accomplished chewers, so be certain that your pet's playthings are chew-proof. Pet shops carry a variety of toys that are suitable for ferrets. Photo by Isabelle Francais.

Ferrets remain young at heart throughout their lifetime. They lose none of their desire to play as they grow older. Photo by Isabelle Francais.

HEALTH

A healthy ferret is easy to spot. The eyes are round and clear. No sign of staining or discharge is visible around the eyes or nose. The nose is moist but not runny. The ferret's body is lithe. The fur is smooth to the touch, lying close to the body. Brushed against its lie, the fur springs back to its normal position. Sores and signs of parasites are not present.

A ferret, just like a dog, can suffer from distemper. Therefore, ask the seller if your prospective pet has received a vaccination for this disease.

HOME ACCOMMODATION

Ferrets kept indoors require very little in the way of housing. A cozy box or cage in which to sleep, with a warm lining, is necessary. A litter tray is also mandatory. An indoor ferret requires its own food and water dishes, just like a cat or dog would.

Those owners with ample indoor space can construct an all-wire pen complete with a nesting compartment and play area. This pen can be placed outdoors during warm weather.

PLAYTHINGS

There is no problem finding toys to amuse a ferret. Balls dangling on a string, bones, cardboard boxes, bits of wood and tubes to scamper through interest a ferret. Be careful about supplying items that your pet could tear apart and swallow. A digestive blockage could be serious trouble.

GROOMING AND BATHING

Ferrets are extremely clean animals. Under normal conditions, they do not require extensive grooming. In fact, some ferrets resent being groomed. Others enjoy the feel of a soft hair brush on their backs.

If your pet should soil itself, sprinkle cornflower, talcum or chalk powder into the coat. Then gently brush it out. A wipe with a silk scarf or chamois leather cloth adds a nice sheen to the fur. Baths can be given on an occasional basis.

HANDLING

To lift a ferret properly, place one hand over its shoulders. Your thumb should pass under the elbow of one leg while the second finger passes under the other. The index finger is placed under the ferret's chin. This hold supports the ferret's body without the need to support its rear legs. Do not lift a pregnant jill in this manner. Her rear legs must be supported with your free hand.

Always talk to your pet when lifting it. Approach it from the front so that it is not taken by surprise. A startled pet is more likely to bite.

SCENT GLANDS

The normal body odor of a ferret is not unpleasant. Indeed, it appeals to some owners. The "infamous" scent glands used in self-defense are really not as powerful as some believe. Even so, a frightened ferret makes use of its scent glands only as a last line of defense.

Feeding

The commercially prepared ferret food available at pet shops should form the bulk of your ferret's diet. Supplement this with canned cat food.

Don't scrimp when it comes to selecting your ferret's food. The little bit of extra money that you may have to spend will ensure that your pet is getting high-quality food that will satisfy its nutritional requirements.

MEAT

Some ferret hobbyists occasionally offer their pet meat scraps. If you feed your ferret meat, always be sure that it is fully cooked.

The meat must come from a reliable source, such as your family butcher. Make a point of purchasing meat that is of the highest degree of freshness.

Your ferret's food dishes should be sturdy, non-tippable, and easy to clean.

There is no need to constantly change your pet's diet. This does not mean, however, that the diet should lack variety. Your ferret will enjoy sampling various kinds of meat tidbits from your table.

FISH

Most ferrets will enjoy a meal of fish, which can be offered as an occasional variation to the regular menu. Choose a non-oily fish such as trout or flounder, and make sure it is de-boned and fully cooked.

VEGETABLES, FRUIT, AND CEREAL

Like people, ferrets vary in their food preferences. Some will go bananas over a piece of fruit, others will turn up their noses at it. The same holds true for the ferret's dietary interest in vegetables and cereal (cornflakes, shredded wheat, and the like).

If your ferret enjoys any of the aforementioned foods, fine. Just remember that they are supplements to its main diet of dried ferret food and should not be served in large quantities.

VITAMINS AND MINERALS

There are a multitude of nutritional supplements on the market today. Caution is the key word here. If you are feeding your pets a varied, wholesome diet, no

Your ferret's diet will be reflected in his overall appearance. Alert, bright-eyed, and plushly coated, this ferret projects every outward sign of good health. Photo by Isabelle Francais.

Ferrets can easily get underfoot and thus be accidentally stepped upon. Attaching a bell to your pet's collar can alert you to the animal's whereabouts and will help prevent such mishaps. Photo by Isabelle Francais.

Your pet may enjoy an occasional nibble of fresh vegetables, but keep in mind that overconsumption can cause digestive disturbance.

vitamin and mineral supplements are necessary. Of course, offering supplements to your pets is a good way to guard against dietary deficiencies. If you are concerned about your pets' diet, consult your veterinarian or a reputable pet shop or breeder.

FEEDING ROUTINE

Wild polecats generally feed at dusk through to dawn. Therefore, the main meal of your pets ideally is given in the evening. A lighter meal should be offered in the morning.

It is best to work out a schedule and stick to it. The ferrets are soon accustomed to a routine. They will await you with eagerness at mealtime.

AVOID SWEETS

Ferrets, like other animals, can become overly fond of foods that are not good for them. Do not give your pets candy, cookies or other sweets. Sticky items should also be avoided.

WATER

Ferrets drink quite a lot of water. It must be fresh every day and available at all times. The drinking water can be supplied via an open dish or, better yet, an automatic gravity-fed dispenser that is attached to the side of the cage. If you choose a dispenser, monitor the ferrets for a time to be sure they know where to find the water.

FOOD DISHES

Probably the best food dishes are earthenware. They are easy to clean and heavy based. The latter feature is important to prevent inadvertent tipping. Plastic dishes are too easily chewed and tossed around.

QUANTITY

Hard and fast rules cannot be laid down. The amount of food offered depends upon a number of factors. The size of the ferret, its appetite, and level of exercise must be taken into consideration. Additionally, ferrets tend to eat less in warm weather (which is no cause for alarm).

The general rule is that your pet should be given only what it can consume in a five-to-ten-minute interval. A pregnant jill requires larger amounts than normal. Also, growing kits consume quite a bit of food.

Breeding

An interesting hobby is ferret breeding. It is also a big responsibility. You must have the time, space and money to devote to a growing colony of ferrets. Before actually breeding, determine what is to be done with the kits—seek out interest among friends and local pet shops.

BREEDING CONDITION

No animal should be expected to reproduce unless it is in top condition. The birth process is particularly demanding on jills. An unfit female is more likely to have problems during pregnancy and birth, and to produce small, weak young.

PHOTOINDUCTION

A ferret is induced into its sexual state by the length of the daylight hours. The male is light-negative, the female light-positive.

During the non-breeding season, the testes of the male recede into his body. They are almost invisible under the heavy winter coat. About the time of the shortest day, his testicles begin to move back into the scrotum. He reaches his sexual peak about March or April. Depending upon the weather in a given year, he remains in a sexual state until the end of the summer. At this time, his testes begin to withdraw back into the body cavity.

The female comes into estrus once the daylight hours begin to increase. She responds to a male when there are about 14 to 15 hours of daylight. Her litter is born, assuming an early mating, in May or June. Now the days are at their longest and warmest.

The kits are weaned at about eight weeks of age. Thus they have autumn to build up their supply of body fat for the coming winter. As the daylight hours shorten, the female goes out of estrus. The breeding cycle is thus completed.

With artificial light to extend daylight hours, it is possible to keep a captive ferret in breeding condition throughout the year. Experts advise against this method. Spring litters are far superior in vigor than those produced during unnatural periods.

A female responds to a male throughout the summer. She is in heat perpetually, not periodically, as are most other female animals. She is induced to ovulate only when stimulated by the presence of a male. Simply the scent of a male is sufficient to induce a jill to ovulate.

An unmated female's estrus ends by early autumn. If she is mated, her estrus terminates at that point until the young are reared.

SEXING

Male ferrets are usually a bit larger than females. The most

Above: A successful ferret breeding program is highly dependent on the selection of the right stock. Photo by Michael Gilroy. **Opposite:** Raising a ferret family requires time and consideration on your part. It also involves your commitment to finding good homes for those ferrets that you don't keep. Photo by Isabelle Francais.

obvious difference, of course, is the sex organs. The testes and anus are some distance apart in the male. The vulva and anus of the female are close together. The testes of the male are obvious in the breeding season. Likewise, the vulva of an unmated jill is dramatically enlarged in size during estrus.

BREEDING AGE

Ferrets attain sexual maturity around six months of age. However, breeding should not be commenced until the young are one year old. Breeding less than fully mature stock results in inferior kits.

MATING

Once you have determined that both ferrets are ready to mate, introduce the jill to the hob's accommodations. The male will chase the female around his home. He will bite her behind the head on the neck. He will attempt to drag her to a sheltered position in order to mate with her. The female may escape a few times. If she is ready to be mated, though, eventually she will go limp. The hob will drag her to a convenient spot, throw her on her side and then mate. The whole process may more resemble a battle than foreplay. The routine may be repeated over a few days. The pair should now be separated.

If the female is not ready to mate at this time, she will make the point clear to the male. Separate the pair. Reintroduce them a few days later.

GESTATION AND BIRTH

The gestation period is 42 days. This can vary a day or two either way. Increase the jill's food intake to allow for the fact that nourishment is being passed to the growing embryos. A dramatic increase in calcium is required for the growing bones of the babies and the lactating period. The jill needs good-quality meat in order to produce vigorous youngsters.

As the birth draws near, the female begins preparing a nest. Supply her with plenty of clean straw. She will also make use of dried leaves and wood shavings.

Do not lift the female during her final stages of pregnancy. The first you should know of the actual birth is when you hear the squeaks of the newborn babies. A typical litter averages six to nine kits. They are born naked, blind and quite helpless.

REARING YOUNGSTERS

Avoid disturbing the nest for two weeks after the babies are born. The female is in a stressful state. The slightest concern for the welfare of her litter may result in her killing them. This is a natural instinct. She would rather do this than have them become a meal to a predator.

The newborns' pink skin is soon covered by white fur. This fur begins to darken in about seven days. The eyes of the kits open when they are about 21 days old.

The babies soon wander about the nest to explore. They are very playful, having mock fights and attacking everything in their reach.

WEANING

By three weeks, the babies will be taking solid meat. They are weaned about six to eight weeks of age. Give them bread and milk to ease the transition to solid food. Puppy meal mixed with finely chopped meat can be offered. They will be eating an adult diet by the time they are ten weeks old.

The ferret youngsters can be left together with the adults. They will live as a small colony unit. At six months of age, though, it is wise to separate the sexes to prevent premature matings. Bear in mind that a jill mated early in the season may come into estrus again. One litter per year is sufficient for any female.

FIRST-LITTER PROBLEMS

The vast majority of females are natural mothers. They have no problems at all. Occasionally, a maiden ferret panics. She may ignore the babies, or even kill and eat them. This jill can be mated again. If the problem reoccurs, however, remove her from the breeding program.

PSEUDOPREGNANCY

Females who have ovulated may not have actually conceived. They may have a false pregnancy. This situation can occur when a female picks up the scent of a male, when she is mated to a sterile hob or simply when she is in the company of pregnant or nursing jills. The female develops as if she were actually pregnant. Her teats may swell. She may even produce milk and build a nest.

HAND-REARING

It may happen that a jill is an unfit mother, becomes ill or dies after giving birth. In such a scenario, it is wise to foster out her kits to other jills with young of their own. Wipe some of the foster mother's urine scent onto the abandoned kits. This lessens the chance of the new mother suspecting that the babies are not hers.

You may not have another female with a litter of similar age. However, this does not mean that someone in your locality does not. This is where being a member of club is really advantageous.

Sometimes it is necessary to hand-rear the kits. This is a tremendous undertaking. It entails bottle feeding the babies every two hours, 24 hours a day.

If you opt to hand-feed, purchase the smallest feeder bottle available. One made for kittens is about right. Feed the youngsters prepared milk for puppies. The milk should be given warm, but not hot.

The kits must be fed every two hours for about three weeks. Gradually cut them down to every three hours, then every four. Human baby meat foods can be offered around 12 days of age. Introduce finely minced meat and chopped egg about the 15th day.

An ID tag is a wise (and inexpensive) investment for your pet. Should he escape his confines, he will be more likely to be returned to you if he is wearing identification. Photo by Isabelle Francais.

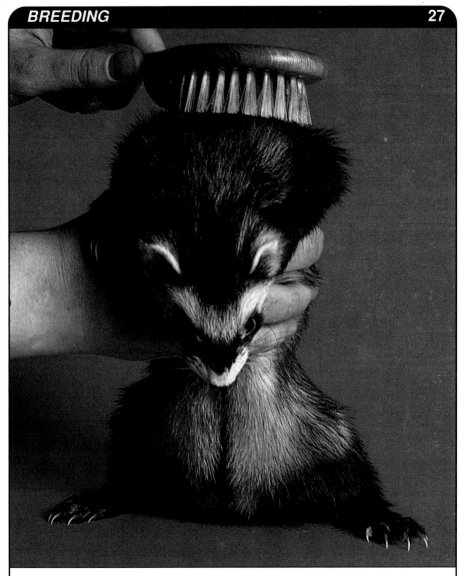

Regular grooming will help to evenly distribute the natural oil in your ferret's coat. Use a soft-bristle brush and a gentle brushing motion. Photo by Isabelle Francais.

Health

A ferret can be as healthy as any other pet. Given adequate housing and a proper diet, it is likely that a ferret will enjoy a life free of accidents and diseases. The greater the number of ferrets kept, however, the greater the risk of introducing and spreading infection. In addition, a ferret can pick up an infection from other animals, such as dogs, cats, and birds.

The key to good husbandry is prevention rather than cure. Examine your pets regularly and thoroughly for any signs of illness. Of course, any ferret can have an off day. Minor ailments, however, do not necessitate panic. Consult a veterinarian for any problem that does not clear in 72 hours. Typically, a pet ferret is treated quite similarly to a cat requiring a vet's attention.

GENERAL CARE

Check the following aspects on a weekly basis.

Teeth: A sloppy, soft-food diet results in food becoming lodged between the teeth. Bacteria is attracted. Likewise, small particles of bone can become embedded in the gums, creating ulcers and abscesses.

Checking a ferret's teeth is a good idea for two reasons. First, the health of their teeth and gums can be ensured. Second, the ferret will become accustomed to your opening its mouth. This is useful should you need to give the ferret a pill or retrieve an item from its clench.

A ferret's teeth can be cleaned with a canine toothpaste. This is not required, however, if the correct diet is supplied.

Ears: Ferrets can attract much the same sort of ear parasites as can dogs and cats. Scratching of the ears is normal. Excessive scratching or carrying the head to one side is not.

The external ear attracts a certain amount of debris. This can be wiped away with a cotton swab soaked in a very mild antiseptic. Do not probe into the ear. If any waxlike substance is visible deeper in the ear, consult your vet. Overzealous cleaning of the ears can precipitate other problems.

Nails: If exercised on hard ground, a ferret's nails will remain at a convenient length. The nails must be trimmed when they begin to curl. This is easily done with a pair of guillotine-type clippers used for dogs. Trim a little at a time. Be careful not to cut the "quick." This is the blood vessel seen at the base of the nail. If the quick should happen to be cut, stop the bleeding with a styptic pencil. If you are nervous about this procedure, let your vet do it rather than risk hurting the ferret.

Skin: Inspect the skin and fur for

parasites and sores. Spikes of grass and straw can lodge in the skin. Any bald patches should be reported immediately to the vet.

Pads: Check the feet pads for any irritation. Again, this has the double advantage of being a health check and getting the ferret used to your holding its feet. Some ferrets enjoy having their pads gently rubbed.

VACCINATIONS

Ferrets are subject to most canine diseases. Fortunately, they can be vaccinated against them. These inoculations include distemper, leptospirosis, hepatitis (not canine), rabies, influenza, enteritis and botulism.

The vaccinations are given around six to ten weeks of age. Annual boosters are recommended. Just how many vaccinations your pet should be given is best discussed with a veterinarian. The doctor should be familiar with those diseases common in your area.

STERILIZATION

Castration is the complete removal of a male's testes. This destroys his sexual drive. It may also reduce the effect of the scent glands. A castrated hob exhibits much less aggression than he normally would during the breeding season. He is less inclined to wander off. Given these advantages, it may be better to sterilize those males purchased solely as pets. The procedure is usually done when the ferret is about six or seven months old.

It is possible to remove a male's scent glands at the same time that he is castrated. This is not recommended, however. Doing so deprives the male of a vital defense mechanism against predators.

A male can also be made infertile by cutting the link between the testes and penis. This prevents the sperm from passing through to the female. The male behaves normally in all other respects. He has the full drive and aggression of a typical male ferret.

A female kept purely as a pet is best spayed. This is a simple operation. The benefit is that all of the attendant risks of estrus are removed.

PARASITES

A ferret can pick up all of the external parasites which infect dogs, cats and rodents. Lice, mites and ticks live by sucking the blood of their hosts. If your dog or cat is being treated for these parasites, then your ferrets and their housing must be treated as well.

Numerous acaricides are available from pet shops. Ticks can be dabbed with petroleum jelly to prompt them to release their hold.

ABSCESSES

Any swelling should be treated with concern. A swelling may be only a localized reaction to an irritation, but it might just as well be a tumor.

A sudden, reddish swelling is likely to be the result of an external

With luck, perhaps your ferret will relish bathtime as much as these two little fellows! An occasional bath will help to keep your ferret looking (and smelling) his best. Photo by Bonnie Buys.

Your ferret's nails should get regular attention. However, be forewarned that most ferrets dislike a manicure. You may find the job easier if someone else holds your ferret while you do the clipping. Photo by Isabelle Francais.

cause, such as a bite or sting. Treat it with a mild antiseptic. Once a swelling has burst, swab it daily. Dust it with an appropriate powder to stop further infection of the wound.

Mouth abscesses are quite common in ferrets. Another area prone to abscess is the anus, especially in unmated jills. Prompt veterinary treatment is required.

DIARRHEA

Normal ferret feces are elongated, moist and firm. The feces will become loose if sloppy or tainted foods are eaten. A stressed ferret will also have loose feces.

Withdraw all food for 24 hours. This should resolve the problem. However, water must still be available at all times. If the feces remain loose, foul-smelling or contain blood, a more serious condition is indicated. Diarrhea is often a symptom of other ailments.

Isolate a ferret with persistent diarrhea. Burn all of its bedding material. The housing must be disinfected thoroughly. If you keep a number of ferrets, it is wise to have a spare accommodation for situations such as this.

Collect a sample of the feces in a suitable container. Take the sample and the ferret to the vet. Microscopy may be the only way to identify the source of the problem.

FLU AND CHILLS

A ferret can catch a cold from you or your other pets. Symptoms resemble those seen in humans—runny eyes and nose, high temperature, loss of appetite and drowsiness. Keep the ferret warm and away from stressful situations. Colds usually clear up quickly.

HEATSTROKE

Ferrets like to bask in the sun. They do not like excess sunshine, however. A ferret can become overheated if it cannot retreat from the sunlight at its own convenience. Therefore, a shaded area must be available to your pet. Never leave any animal in a closed car on a hot day.

A ferret suffering from heatstroke pants and becomes lethargic. It needs immediate attention. Quickly take it to a cool spot.

The ferret can be dipped in cool water. (The water must not be cold; too rapid a change in temperature may result in shock.) Submerge the body, but be sure to hold the ferret's head above the water line. The head can be stroked with the cool water.

Once the ferret appears to be reviving, towel it down. Place the animal in a cool, dry spot. The area must be free from drafts to avoid a chill.

SHOCK

The symptoms of shock much resemble heatstroke. Shock can be induced by loud, sudden noise. A chase by a predator or any similar, sudden movement may also induce shock. Be aware that the shock may not be instant—there may be a delay from the time of the incident to the onset of shock.

Place an animal suffering from shock in a warm, quiet spot. Speak softly and gently stroke the ferret. Recovery is normally rapid after some attention and a favored tidbit.

SUDDEN DEATH

Occasionally an animal dies quite suddenly, without exhibiting any clinical signs of illness. It is wise to have your vet conduct a post mortem to establish the cause of death. You should know whether the cause was genetic, due to poor husbandry or contagious in nature so that these factors can be corrected.

WOUNDS

Wounds may be a daily occurrence for active, inquisitive ferrets. All wounds should be carefully swabbed to establish their extent. Minor abrasions need little attention beyond cleansing with a mild antiseptic. More serious cuts must be cleaned. A dressing must be placed on the wound and the ferret taken to a vet.

QUARANTINE

A period of quarantine is mandatory before introducing any new ferret to an established stock. Failure to do so is taking an unnecessary risk, regardless of how good the source of supply. A minimum of ten days of isolation must be allowed to permit any incubating illness to show itself.

Bibliography

FERRETS
By Wendy Winsted, M. D.
ISBN 0-86622-829-2
T.F.H. KW-074
Contents: Introduction. Choosing Your Ferret. Handling. Feeding Your Ferret. Housebreaking. Ferret Grooming. Ferret Health. Ferret Reproductive Systems. Breeding and Birth. Ferret Play and Personality.
Hard cover, 5½ x 8", completely illustrated with full-color photos and drawings. 128 pages.

FERRETS AND FERRETING
By Graham Wellstead
ISBN 0-86622-988-1
T.F.H. PS-792
Contents: Introduction. The Mysterious Ferret. Confining the Brutes—Housing. To Satisfy the Inner Ferret—Feeding. The Ever-Increasing Horde—Breeding. The Hunt Is on—Working. Net Making. Ferreting and the Law. In Sickness and Health—Ailments.
Hard cover, 5½ x 8", 192 pages, 17 full-color photos, 28 black and white photos.

FERRETS IN YOUR HOME
By Wendy Winsted, M.D.
ISBN 0-86622-988-4
T.F.H. TS-106
Contents: Introduction. Choosing Your Ferret. Temperament and Handling. Preparing for Arrival. Feeding Your Ferret. Housebreaking. Ferret Grooming. Ferret Health. Reproduction System. Breeding. Safety. Traveling with Your Ferret. Becoming a Two-Ferret Family. Ferrets and Other Animals. Ferret Lessons.
Hard cover, 5½ x 8½", 192 pages, over 90 full-color photos and drawings.